Follow Your Nose

11/06

FOLLOW YOUR NOSE

DISCOVER YOUR SENSE

OF

SMELL

VICKI COBB

Illustrated by

Cynthia C. Lewis

The Millbrook Press Brookfield, Connecticut

The author takes full responsibility for the accuracy
of the text, and gratefully acknowledges Marci Pelchat, Ph.D.,
and Pam Dalton, Ph.D., of the Monell Chemical Senses
Center for their creative contributions and review of portions
of the manuscript. Also, thanks to Marian Strasser for an
introduction to vinaigrettes.

Published by The Millbrook Press, Inc.
2 Old New Milford Road
Brookfield, CT   06804
www.millbrookpress.com.

Library of Congress Cataloging-in-Publication Data
Cobb, Vicki.
Follow your nose : discover your sense of smell / Vicki Cobb;
illustrations by Cynthia C. Lewis.
p.   cm.
Summary: Examines the sense of smell, how the nose detects
different odors, and how we react to different smells. Includes
simple experiments to test the sense of smell.
ISBN 0-7613-1521-7 (lib. bdg.)
1. Smell—Juvenile literature. [1. Smell. 2. Senses and sensation.]
I. Lewis, Cynthia Copeland, 1960– II. Title.
QP458.C62   2000   612.8'6—dc21   99-047872

Stick your nose into this book and sniff. Smell anything? If you do, it probably isn't very strong, and after a few seconds you can't smell it anymore. A room full of books has a stronger smell. Ever notice the smell in a library or a bookstore? If you were blindfolded, do you think your nose would know when you were in a hardware store, or a drugstore, or a supermarket?

COMMUNITY BULLETIN BOARD

- TONIGHT!
Softball
Championships
the Rockin'
Raccoons
VS.
the Powerful
Porcupines

FOR SALE
HOUSEHOLD
GOODS.
MUST
SHARE!
OWNER
RETIRING TO
FLORIDA.
Call Doc at
551-5213

- BOBCAT FAMILIES -
SEPT. 24th
Potluck Supper
BRING A DEAD ANIMAL
TO SHARE!
(Please put your name
on your dishes!)

TONIGHT'S MOVIE
AT THE COLLEGE.
A real SMELL BINDER!
"Scents and
Scents-ability"
ALL SKUNKS WELCOME

- BEAR CUB SCOUTS
Meeting: Thurs., 7 p.m.
TOPIC:
GOLDILOCKS:
Friend or foe?

- LOST:
Sheep
Call Little Bo
Peep at
489-8694

STINKERS
Important
Meeting!!
Tonight 7 p.m.
At the Clubhouse
Refreshments
Provided!

Know how to stop smelling? Hold your nose. You can breathe through your mouth, but you can smell only when air passes through your nose. Your nose is constructed so that air swirls as it moves through your nostrils. It is easier to detect odors in swirling air than in smoothly flowing air. That's why you sniff when you're not sure of a smell. Sniffing makes the air swirl more.

The swirling air arrives at a large cavelike space at the back of the nose. On the ceiling of this cavity, just under the bridge of your nose, is your organ of smell. It is a patch of mucus-covered skin, about the size of a postage stamp, containing about 8 million tiny nerve endings. (The mucus keeps the skin moist and protects it from germs.) The nerves travel directly to the brain through the bottom of the skull, which has many tiny holes for the nerves to pass through.

If you think you've got a lot of nerves, compare yourself to a really good smeller like a dog. A sheepdog has about 220 million nerve endings in its organ of smell!

Taste and smell are called "chemical senses" because they need certain chemicals to make your nerves fire and send messages to your brain. The smallest pieces of chemicals are called *molecules*. You can't see molecules even with the strongest microscope, but your nerves can detect them. Sugar and salt molecules make nerves in your tongue fire. Molecules in the air reach your organ of smell and make your smelling nerves fire. When a nerve fires, a message travels up the nerve to your brain. It's the brain's job to recognize the smell so you know how to react to it.

Ralph tries to fool his brain

* SNIFF *
* SNIFF *

Yummy Cookie →

← Yucky dead fish

A lot of air passes over your organ of smell every day. It takes about two seconds to inhale and three seconds to exhale, so you breathe about 23,040 times every day. This is about as much as the amount of air in an average-size bathroom. With every breath your sense of smell checks out the air, ready to detect odors.

Scientists guess that there are about 400,000 different kinds of smelly molecules. Human beings learn between 3,000 and 10,000 of them. In many ways, smell is a mystery still being studied by scientists. You can be a scientist and make your own study of smell. This book tells you how.

I CAN'T go to bed YET! I still have to take 38 more breaths!

Benjamin's parents wish he didn't take things quite so literally.

These Smells Are DELICIOUS

why the girls don't sit with Herm and Phil at lunch.

ha ha ha!!

If it smells good enough to eat, it probably is. Your sense of smell gives most of the flavor to food. That's because your nose and your mouth are connected. Want proof? When you laugh while you're drinking milk, the milk comes out your nose.

If food didn't taste good, you might not eat it, and without eating you would starve. When you have a cold, you can't smell your food, and it is not as tasty. People who have lost their sense of smell through an injury or a disease complain that they don't enjoy eating the way they used to.

If you can't smell a food, it's hard to tell what it is. Experiment to test this out. Prepare a half-inch cube of a potato, an apple, and an onion. Put on a blindfold and nose clips. Have a friend place one of the cubes on the middle of your tongue without telling you which one it is. Don't chew it or move it around your mouth. Can you guess correctly which it is? Take off the nose clips. Now can you tell? With a blindfold and nose clips it's hard to tell the difference between a cola and a clear lemon-lime drink or between a cherry and a grape jelly bean. Try it and see.

Ever notice the smell of dinner when you first come home? Take a deep breath and inhale the aroma. Yum! It's enough to get the juices flowing. Now take another deep breath. Can you still smell it? How many deep breaths before you can no longer smell the aroma no matter how much you sniff?

The reason you stop noticing the smell is that your nerves get tired. Scientists call this *adaptation.* Your sense of smell adapts very quickly. It recovers when you go someplace else where the odor molecules can't reach you. Then when you return, you notice the smell again.

when you first come home...

10 minutes later...

Katie's Science Notes

Do an **experiment** to see how your sense of smell adapts:
→ YOU WILL NEED:

2 small containers
vanilla extract
VAN

ground cinnamon
measuring spoons

➡ In one container, mix one teaspoon of ground cinnamon with four teaspoons of vanilla extract. In the other container, mix one teaspoon of ground cinnamon with four teaspoons of water.

Sniff the cinnamon-vanilla mixture until you can't smell it anymore. It will take at least six sniffs. Then immediately sniff the cinnamon-water mixture until you can't smell it. Immediately sniff the cinnamon-vanilla mixture again.

me, sniffing ↘

The <u>second</u> time you smell the cinnamon-vanilla mixture, it should smell different from the first time. This time it will smell more like <u>VANILLA</u> than <u>CINNAMON</u>.

Goofy boy sitting next to me!

HERE'S WHAT HAPPENED.

When you sniffed the cinnamon-vanilla mixture, you tired out the nerves that respond to BOTH smells.

tired
nerves →

ho hum

Then when you sniffed the cinnamon-water mixture, you only tired the nerves that respond to CINNAMON. When you returned to the cinnamon-vanilla mixture, the nerves that smell vanilla had recovered → while the nerves that smell cinnamon were still tired. →

AS A RESULT, you only smelled VANILLA.

This shows that different nerves react to different kinds of smells.

yummy smell

icky smell

sweet smell

Perfume

GROSS SMELL

JOSH

noxious

overpower with stink

bad odor

offensive

fume

smoke

hold one's nose

stink

Personal Portable Stench Protection

Throughout the ages people have found ways to avoid bad odors. Sweet-smelling woods called incense were burned at funerals so that people didn't have to smell the dead. Perfumes disguised the smell of unwashed bodies and clothes. One particularly clever invention was carried by English ladies and gentlemen two hundred years ago. It was a tiny silver box with a hinged cover, called a *vinaigrette* (vin-a-GRET). Inside was some cloth that had been soaked in a mixture of vinegar and spices. When a person got a whiff of a stench, out came the vinaigrette. A long, deep breath of stinging vinegar and herbs was enough to destroy the foul air.

stink like a pig

armpit

bad smell

reek

runk

stink-pot

stench

foul

You can make your own version of a vinaigrette.

YOU WILL NEED:

an empty plastic dental-floss box
scissors
a clean kitchen sponge
a saucer

white vinegar
ground cinnamon
ground nutmeg
measuring spoons

Cut a piece of sponge to fit into the dental floss-box. Put a tablespoon of white vinegar, a half teaspoon of cinnamon and a half teaspoon of nutmeg in a saucer. Mix thoroughly. Soak the piece of sponge in the vinegar-spice mixture. Put it into the dental-floss box and close the cover.

Carry your vinaigrette around with you. When you encounter a bad smell, flip open the top and sniff.

ANNOUNCING
VINAIGRETTE
the latest advancement in
Personal Portable Stench Protection
Are you *tired* of being grossed out by...
Filthy pigs
Rotten eggs
Armpits
Dead fish
Icky breath
Sweaty feet
Horse manure
Litter boxes
stifle those nasty odors
just $19.95 plus $4.95 shipping and handling
CALL TODAY!
1-800-NO STINK

These Smells Are A Defense

When threatened, a skunk lifts its tail and directs a stream of powerful, smelly liquid toward its enemy. If you get a direct hit, you may start retching, and your eyes will burn. Days later you will still be able to smell its very distinctive foul odor. No, you don't want to mess with a skunk!

The skunk's smelly weapon is a mixture of about seven different oils. It is so strong that you can smell it even if there are only ten molecules of it in every billion molecules of air. If you are upstairs and a skunk sprays downstairs at the other end of the house, you will smell it within seconds.

Gardeners protect their plants from deer by sprinkling them with a smell that deer find unpleasant. There is also a smelly spray to prevent people from chopping down evergreens for Christmas trees. Outside you don't notice the spray. But if you bring the tree inside where it's warm, the room soon fills with a disagreeable odor. Naturally, there is a sign to warn tree thieves.

These Smells Are a Warning!

Have no fear! SUPERMAN is here!

No! Super NOSE is here!

Your sense of smell can save your life!

Your nose is in direct contact with your surroundings, so if there is danger in the air, you can detect it. You are not born knowing what danger smells like. But you learn quickly that the smell of smoke where there is not supposed to be a fire tells you to move quickly.

Some dangerous gases have no smell. Carbon monoxide is the result of burning where there is not enough oxygen. People have died from carbon-monoxide poisoning when running their cars in a closed garage or when using a kerosene heater in a small, closed cabin or tent. Home carbon-monoxide detectors are recommended in case a problem develops with the furnace.

Like carbon monoxide, natural gas has no smell. An overexposure to it can kill you. So gas companies add to the gas a smelly chemical called methyl mercaptan. You would never be able to detect a gas leak without methyl mercaptan. Our noses are so sensitive to this chemical that you only need one part of methyl mercaptan in 25 trillion parts of air in order to smell it and call the gas company.

A lifesaving SUPER HERO

These Smells are enjoyable

What smells do you like? Flowers, freshly baked pie, perfume, clean laundry, your mother, pine needles, popcorn, leather, shampoo? Lots of time and money are spent on making things smell good. Go on a fragrance hunt around your house. How many good smells can you sniff out?

By the way, just because something has a wonderful aroma doesn't mean it's good enough to eat. Vanilla extract and perfume both smell terrific and taste awful.

The first smell a baby learns to love is his or her mother. Every person has a special smell. Do you know the smell of your mother? You can do an experiment with your friends to find out. Get everyone to bring a cotton shirt their mother has worn for a day in a paper bag. One person puts on a blindfold. Another person holds each shirt, one at a time, under the nose of the blindfolded guesser. Can he or she detect the right shirt by smell alone?

You can make a wonderful-smelling, old-fashioned, spice-and-citrus decoration called a *pomander*. You will need a small thin-skinned orange or tangerine and a box of whole cloves. Stick the pointed end of a clove through the skin of the orange. It should go in easily, but if your hands are not strong enough, you can make a hole with a ballpoint pen and then stick the clove into this hole. Keep inserting cloves through the skin of the fruit. You can put the cloves next to each other so that you can no longer see the surface of the fruit or you can put the cloves in a pattern.

"Look at the pattern I made with my cloves!"

Put the pomander someplace to dry. It will take up to three weeks. You can tie a ribbon around the pomander and hang it in a closet, or you can put it in a drawer to make your clothes smell wonderful. The orange doesn't rot because it is dry and because cloves contain a chemical that discourages mold and bacteria from growing.

Use Your Nose

Could you tell what something is by smell alone? Do an experiment to find out.

YOU WILL NEED:

several plastic film canisters (you can get them free from film-processing stores)
odorless gauze
scissors
rubber bands
small labels

Small items that smell such as: bubble gum, popcorn, crayons, pencil shavings, a Band-Aid, Play-Dough, toothpaste, coffee, dirt, orange peel, pine needles, mothballs, rose petals.

Place each smelly item inside its own film canister. Cover the top with a square of gauze and hold it in place with a rubber band. Write the name of the contents on a label and stick it to the bottom of the canister.

Have a friend sniff each canister and see if he or she can name what's in it.

Was anyone 100 percent correct? How many times did your subject say, "I know what it is, but I don't remember its name?" Also ask your sniffer if the smell brings up memories from the past and what the memories are. You might be surprised at the memories some adults come up with.

It is very common for a person to remember a smell without remembering its name. That's because of where our senses connect to our brain. Your sense of sight is located in the same part of the brain that language comes from. So what you see is directly linked to its name. But smell is connected to a part of the brain that is responsible for emotions, not language. The connection in the brain between a smell and its name is not as direct, so people have more difficulty naming a smell they are sure they know.

Since smell and memory are so close, smells can bring back memories of times and places in the past that people have forgotten.

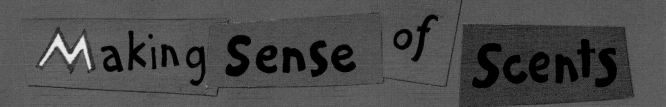

Making Sense of Scents

Is there a way to sort out the thousands of different smells humans can detect? Several people have tried to figure out a system.

dog breath smell

scientist →

Soggy Zwieback Cracker and poopy diaper smell

stuff left for 8 months in a gym locker smell

Lustre Creme
LOTION SHAMPOO

Sitting behind old ladies in church smell

just washed hair smell

Grandma's house during the holidays smell

first thing in the morning smell

No system has the final word. One list says that there are seven basic smells, and all the others are variations and combinations of these seven. You can make your own kit of basic smells.

seven little plastic film canisters with their caps
some adhesive labels and a pen

a hammer
a nail
a block of wood

On the block of wood, make 7 holes in each of the caps with the nail and hammer.

Make labels as shown below and put one on each canister. Put a sample of the smelly material in the canister and put on the cap.

Label	Sample
Camphoric	A mothball
Musky	Aftershave lotion on a piece of sponge
Floral	Rose petals or some other sweet-smelling flower
Pepperminty	Slightly chewed mint gum
Ethereal	Nail-polish remover on a piece of sponge
Pungent	Vinegar on a piece of sponge
Putrid	A piece of Limburger or Roquefort cheese

Now you can go around sniffing other smells and compare them with the smells in your sense kit. Then you can say, "It smells like. . . . "

A Talented Nose

Some people are better smellers than others. They remember what they sniff. They can tell when an odor is a combination of scents, and they can name the different parts. People like this can work for a company that makes perfumes and other scents that are sold to manufacturers of cosmetics and household products.

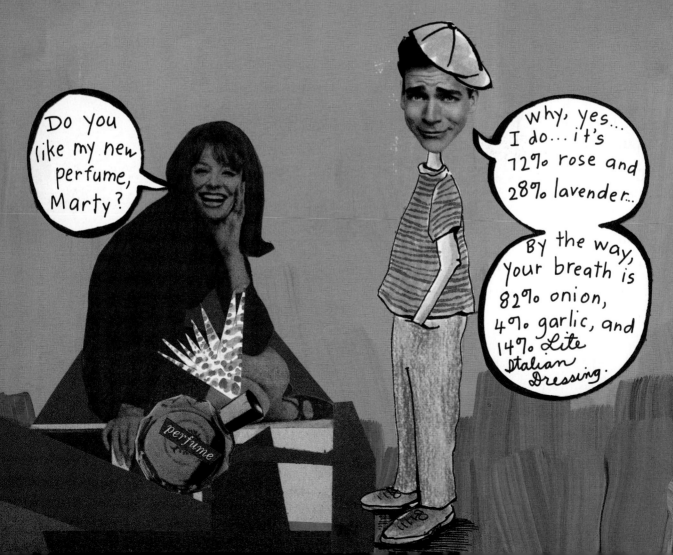

A person who creates perfumes is called a "nose."
A nose is an expert on fragrances. He or she learns
how to describe them.

I'm a
teacher...
And, let's
see... you
are a...

Go
ahead...
GUESS!
You'll never
get it!

Do you think you could be a nose? Sniff
some perfume. Is it flowery? Is it like oranges? Is it
like spices? Can you remember a perfume and
name it?

The only way to find out if your nose is
talented is to use it.

ABOUT THE AUTHOR

Vicki Cobb has a nose for science fun. She is always
sniffing around to find the most interesting ways to do
science. In this book, she'll make you want to stick
your nose into all sorts of places because that's the
best way to have fun with your sense of smell.
Visit Vicki at www.vickicobb.com

ABOUT THE ILLUSTRATOR

Using her highly tuned sense of fun, Cynthia Lewis
sniffed out photos from old magazines to illustrate
this series of books. Cindy's favorite smells are warm
chocolate chip cookies, elementary schools, a fall day
right before it snows, and her grandmother's perfume.